STARTERS
PEOPLE

Scott and Amundsen

Macdonald Educational

These children are visiting a ship.
It is called the Discovery.
The Discovery sailed to the Antarctic.
The Antarctic is the coldest land
in the world.

Long ago men sailed to the Antarctic.
They tried to reach the South Pole.
Thick ice floated in the sea.
Their ships were not strong enough
to push through the ice.

Robert Scott was an Englishman.
He led an expedition to the Antarctic.
He and his men sailed in the Discovery.
They learned to travel over snow and ice.
They studied rocks and animals.

4

Scott decided to make another expedition.
He wanted to be the first man
to reach the South Pole.
He said goodbye to his friends.

Scott went to New Zealand.
He and his men loaded a ship
with food, sledges and tools.

6

skis

They took dogs and ponies too.
The ship was called the Terra Nova.

igloo

husky
dogs

Amundsen was a Norwegian explorer.
He visited the Eskimos in the Arctic.
He learned how to live in cold lands.
He wanted to be the first man
to reach the North Pole.

8

port in Madeira

telegram

Another man, called Peary, got there first.
So Amundsen decided to go
to the South Pole instead.
He sent a telegram to Scott,
to tell him of his change of plan.

The Terra Nova

Scott thought Amundsen might reach
the South Pole first.
But Scott decided to go there anyway.
His ship pushed its way through the ice.
10

motor sledge

Scott set up camp in the Antarctic.
His men built a hut to live in.

store
room

Amundsen arrived ten days after Scott.
He set up his camp.
This camp was a long way from Scott.
Amundsen dug underground store rooms.

12

Amundsen stayed in camp all winter.
He made preparations for his journey
to the South Pole.
Some of his men went seal hunting.

diary

Scott did not go to the South Pole at once.
He also spent the winter in camp.
He had to wait for better weather.
His men had lots of jobs to do.
Scott kept a diary about them.

14

weather
balloon

camera

One man took photographs.
Some of the men studied the weather.
Other men caught fish through holes
in the ice.

Some of Scott's men studied penguins.
These penguins are called Emperor penguins.

16

Scott's party

cairn

The summer came.
The days were light and warmer.
Both explorers set off to the South Pole.
Amundsen set off first.

17

Scott's party was caught in a snowstorm.
They built a high wall
to protect themselves.
They had to stay in their tents
for several days.

18

All Scott's ponies died.
Scott and his men had to pull
the sledges themselves.
They climbed a high glacier.

husky dogs

Amundsen reached the South Pole first.
His journey had been easier.
Strong dogs pulled his sledges.
Amundsen put up the Norwegian flag.

A few weeks later, Scott arrived.
He saw footsteps in the snow.
He knew Amundsen had got there first.
He found a letter for him in Amundsen's tent.

21

On the journey back to Scott's camp
the weather turned very cold.
One man, called Oates, became very ill.
He walked out into the snow on purpose.
He was never seen again.

rocks

A few days later, Scott and his friends
died of cold and hunger.
A rescue party found them in their tent.
They found Scott's diary.
This is how we know about his journey.

Amundsen reached his camp safely.
He went home to Norway.

airship

polar
bear

Amundsen continued his explorations.
He was the first man to fly
over the North Pole in an airship.

card

match box

glue

clay

string

See if you can make a sledge like this.

26

Index

**Food rations for one man
for one day
(Scott's party)**

butter

pemmican

biscuits

cocoa

sugar

tea

Some explorers of the Antarctic

1839–43   Sir James Ross discovered the Ross Sea.

1897–99   Adrien de Gerlache drifted for twelve months in the
          pack ice. His ship was the first exploring ship
          to winter in the Antarctic.

1901–4   Scott's expedition to the Antarctic in the Discovery.

1911   Amundsen reached the South Pole.

1912   Scott reached the South Pole.

1929   Richard Byrd flew over the South Pole.

1955–58   Vivian Fuchs crossed the Antarctic continent
          from the Weddell Sea to the Ross Sea.